This book belongs to:

Эта книга принадлежит:

For Keano, Teanna and Ronomi,
my precious children

I Am The Gingerbread Man

Я – пряничный человечек

English-Russian Bilingual Book for Children

Книга для детей на английском и русском языках

Based on the fairy tale *"The Gingerbread Man"*

Illustrated by Olga Ritchie

Written and translated by Olga Ritchie

This is a gingerbread man.

Это - пряничный

человечек.

He likes **to run.**

Он любит **бегать.**

He likes
to run
fast.

Он любит
бегать
быстро.

We can't **catch** him.

Мы не можем его **поймать.**

He is **fast.**

Он **быстрый.**

He is **very** fast.

Он **очень**

быстрый.

"You can't catch me"

"Run, run as fast as you can. You can't catch me. I am the Gingerbread man."

"Быстрее всех могу я бежать. Я - пряничный человечек. Меня не поймать."

gingerbread man

ПРЯ-НИЧ-НЫЙ
ЧЕ-ЛО-ВЕ-ЧЕК

fast

БЫ-СТРЫЙ

He likes to run.

ОН ЛЮ-БИТ БЕ-ГАТЬ

The End

Конец

Printed in Great Britain
by Amazon